ZERO TO CODE

A Fun and Easy Guide to Master Programming from Scratch

OM SINHA

Disclaimer

This book, "Zero to Code: A Fun and Easy Guide to Master Programming from Scratch," is designed to introduce readers to the fundamental principles of programming. The primary goal is to equip beginners with a solid understanding of programming concepts, problem-solving skills, and algorithmic thinking that can be applied across various programming languages and scenarios.

While Python is used throughout this book as the primary language for illustrating these concepts, this book is not intended to serve as a complete guide to Python programming. It focuses on core programming principles that are transferable to other languages, enabling readers to build a strong foundation for their programming journey.

Readers seeking an in-depth exploration of Python syntax, libraries, and advanced features should refer to dedicated Python resources and handbooks. This book aims to inspire and empower readers to take their first steps into the world of programming with confidence.

Image Credits:

The images and illustrations used throughout this book were obtained from Freepik.com, a platform offering royalty-free resources. Credit for these images goes to their respective creators. The author acknowledges and appreciates their contribution to the visual presentation of this book.

"The people who are crazy enough to think they can change the world are the ones who do." – Steve Jobs

Introduction

Welcome to the exciting journey of coding! If you've ever wondered what it's like to bring ideas to life through programming, you've picked up the right book. Zero to Code - A Fun and Easy Guide to Master Programming from Scratch, is designed for absolute beginners—those who might feel a little intimidated by the thought of coding but are eager to learn.

You might be asking yourself: "Why should I learn to code?" The answer is simple: coding is a superpower that allows you to solve problems, automate tasks, and create things from scratch. Imagine having the ability to build an app that helps you organize your grocery list or a program that reminds you when it's time for chai breaks. With coding, the possibilities are endless!

But let's be honest. The world of programming can feel a bit overwhelming at first, especially with all the jargon and technical terms that often accompany it. That's why we're here—to take it step by step, keeping it fun, engaging, and relatable. We'll break down complex concepts into digestible bites, ensuring that you not only learn but also enjoy the process.

In this book, you'll discover:

- The **basics of programming**—what it is and why it matters.

- How to choose a beginner-friendly programming language (spoiler alert: we'll be using Python!).

- The tools you need to set up your coding environment.

- Simple, hands-on exercises to reinforce what you learn.

Whether you're a college student, a fresh graduate, or simply someone who wants to explore the tech world, this book is your friendly guide to becoming a confident coder. No prior experience is needed; all you need is a curious mind and a willingness to learn!

And remember, this isn't just about writing lines of code. It's about **developing a mindset** that embraces creativity and problem-solving. Learning to code can open doors to various opportunities, from developing apps to working on exciting projects. Even if you don't envision yourself as a full-time programmer, the skills you gain will benefit you in countless ways, both personally and professionally.

So, grab your laptop, and let's embark on this adventure together! By the end of this book, you'll not only understand the core principles of programming but also be well on your way to writing your very own code. Let's get started on this journey from **zero to code**!

The Book is Dedicated to

❈

To Dad,

This book wouldn't exist without the spark you ignited. Remember that curious kid peeking through computer shop window, captivated by the magic of computers? That was me, fueled by a dream that seemed out of reach. Thank you for believing in that dream, for squeezing every penny to get me into that first computer class. Your unwavering support laid the foundation for this journey.

To Mr. Amitava Ganguly and
Mr. Sandipan Chakravorty,

My deepest gratitude to the teachers who saw the potential beyond the nine-year-old me. Thank you, Mr. Ganguly, for introducing me to the world of computer studies and igniting my passion for code. And Mr. Chakravorty, your patience with my endless questions and your dedication to explaining complex concepts in a way I could understand made a lasting impact.

This book is dedicated to all of you, my guiding lights on this incredible coding adventure.

Contents

## Chapter 1

Welcome to the World of Code

Why Learn to Code?

Let's be real for a moment. You've probably heard that coding is something only brilliant minds with high IQs can do. Well, **that's not true at all**. Coding isn't some magical skill reserved for geniuses in labs. Coding is for **everyone**, including you.

It doesn't matter if you're a college student, a recent grad, or someone who's never thought about writing code before—**you can learn to code**. It's not rocket science (unless, of course, you're coding for a rocket, but that's a whole other story!). Coding is a skill anyone can pick up, and the best part is, it's **fun**.

You might be thinking, "Why should I bother learning to code if I don't want to be a programmer?" That's a great question! Even if you don't plan on pursuing a career in programming, coding helps you develop some pretty awesome skills. For starters, it teaches you **problem-solving** and **out-of-the-box thinking**—skills that are super useful in everyday life.

Think about it this way: Coding is a way of breaking down big problems into smaller, more manageable parts. Let's say your goal is to organize a family trip. Instead of getting overwhelmed by all the details, you break it into steps—picking a destination, setting a budget, planning activities, and so on. That's exactly how coding works!

So, whether you're coding an app or organizing your life, these skills will serve you well. Plus, once you get the hang of it, coding is like solving puzzles—it can actually be fun!

Debunking the Myths around Programming

Before we dive into the world of code, let's clear up some misconceptions about programming that might have been floating around.

Myth #1: Coding is Too Difficult

You might have heard that coding is this impossible, difficult-to-master skill. But honestly, if you've ever followed a recipe to cook something (like your favorite masala chai), you already know the basics of coding. Coding is simply following steps—do this, then do that, and voila, you've got results! Start small, and take it one step at a time. The key is to be patient with yourself.

Myth #2: You Need to Be Good at Math

Ah yes, the old "coding = math" myth. This one has scared away so many people. But the truth is, coding isn't all about math. Sure, if you're working on complex algorithms, you might need some math skills. But for the majority of what you'll be doing (especially as a beginner), coding is more about **logic and creativity** than crunching numbers. It's like playing a game of chess—you're strategizing, thinking ahead, and solving problems.

Myth #3: Only Computer Science Students Can Learn to Code

Guess what? You don't need a fancy computer science degree to code. In fact, many of the best coders out there are self-taught. With the vast amount of resources available today, anyone with a passion for learning can pick up coding. You've already taken the first step by picking up this book!

Myth #4: Coding Requires Expensive Equipment

Some people think that to code, you need the latest, most powerful laptop or fancy tech gadgets. But here's the truth: **you don't need an expensive setup** to get started with coding. A simple, reliable computer is more than enough to write code and run programs. In fact, some people even start learning on their smartphones! What matters most is your desire to learn, not the hardware you're working on.

Myth #5: You Need to Spend Years Learning Before You Can Do Anything Useful

This one can really discourage beginners. Many people think they need to study programming for years before they can build anything meaningful. That's simply not true! You can write your first useful program much sooner than you think. From automating small tasks (like renaming files) to creating basic apps (like a calculator or to-do list), you'll be building practical things before you know it. Coding is all about applying what you've learned right away, so don't worry about needing to be an expert before seeing results.

Coding as a Superpower: Real-Life Impact

Now, let's talk about the impact coding can have in the real world. In many ways, coding is like having a superpower. It allows you to **create things from scratch**, automate everyday tasks, and solve problems in ways you never thought possible.

Think about the apps and websites you use every day. Whether it's ordering food, booking a cab, or even paying your bills online—**someone, somewhere, wrote**

the code that powers those apps. And here's the fun part: the people who built those apps? They started just like you—by learning the basics of programming.

Coding doesn't have to be all about building the next billion-dollar startup. Sometimes it's about making your life a little easier. You can write a small program to **automate repetitive tasks**, like sending out reminder emails or keeping track of your expenses. Coding gives you the power to create solutions for everyday problems.

Want a real-life example? Let's say you love chai (who doesn't, right?). Imagine you have a little recipe app that helps you adjust the ingredients based on the number of people. Or maybe you want to write a program that sends you an alert when it's time to steep the tea. These small programs might not change the world, but they'll definitely add some spice to your life—pun intended!

So, get ready to unlock your coding superpowers. Even if you don't become the next tech mogul, you'll learn how to solve problems and think in ways that are applicable to almost everything you do.

Conclusion: Let's Start Coding!

Welcome to the world of code! The goal of this book is to make learning programming **simple, fun**, and **accessible** to everyone—whether you want to become a full-time coder or just learn something new for fun.

In the next chapters, I'll walk you through the basics of coding. From learning what a programming language is to writing your very first line of code, we're going to break it down step by step.

Ready? Let's dive in and get coding!

## Chapter 2

The Language of Computers

Now that we've cleared up some of the myths and explored why coding is such a powerful skill, it's time to dive deeper into what you'll actually be doing: writing code. But how do you "talk" to a computer? Well, the secret lies in something called a **programming language**.

What is a Programming Language?

In simple terms, a programming language is the way we communicate with computers. Think of it like learning a new spoken language—except instead of talking to humans, you're giving instructions to machines. Just like you use English, Hindi, or Tamil to communicate with people, you use Python, Java, or C++ to communicate with computers.

The computer doesn't understand human languages, so we need to write our instructions in a way it can process. Programming languages help translate human ideas into a format computers can understand. But don't worry—most modern programming languages (like Python) are very readable and closer to English than you'd expect.

How Do Computers Understand Code?

When you write code, the computer doesn't directly understand the words and sentences you type. Instead, it uses something called a **compiler** or an **interpreter** to translate your code into **machine language**—a series of 1s and 0s (binary code). This is the only language that computers truly understand.

Think of it like this: When you give instructions to someone who speaks a different language, you might need a translator. In the same way, your code is translated into something the computer can understand. That's why programming languages are designed to be readable by humans but can still be translated into machine instructions.

Choosing a Beginner-Friendly Programming Language (Why Python?)

There are hundreds of programming languages out there, each designed for different types of tasks. Some are better for building websites, others for apps or video games. But when you're just starting out, it's important to pick a language that's easy to learn and widely used.

Enter **Python**—one of the most beginner-friendly programming languages out there. Python is like the "English" of programming languages. Its syntax (the way you write the code) is clean, easy to understand, and very close to plain English. Python is used in various fields, from web development to data science, artificial intelligence, and more. By learning Python, you'll gain a foundation that can take you in many different directions.

Plus, Python has a huge community of learners and professionals, so you'll always find resources, tutorials, and forums to help you if you get stuck.

Setting Up Your Coding Environment (Python + VS Code)

Now that we've chosen Python as our language, let's set up everything we need to start coding. We'll be using two essential tools:

1. **Python** itself, which is the language.

2. **VS Code** (Visual Studio Code), which is a great editor where you'll write and run your Python programs.

Don't worry, I'll guide you through the installation process step-by-step.

Step 1: Installing Python

First, let's install Python on your computer. Follow these steps:

1. **Go to the official Python website:**

   Open your browser and go to the official Python downloads page:

   ```
   https://www.python.org/downloads/.
   ```

2. **Download the installer:**

    You'll see a big yellow button that says **Download Python 3.x.x** (the "x.x" might be a different number depending on the latest version). Click on that button to start downloading the installer.

3. **Run the installer:**

    Once the download is complete, open the installer. You'll see an option that says **Add Python to PATH**—make sure to check this box before proceeding!

4. **Install Python:**

    Now, click **Install Now** and wait for the installation to complete. After installation, you should see a success message. Congratulations! You now have Python installed on your machine.

Step 2: Installing VS Code

Next, let's set up Visual Studio Code (VS Code), a lightweight and powerful code editor that will make writing and running your Python programs a breeze.

1. **Download VS Code:**

    Head over to the official VS Code website:

    ```
    https://code.visualstudio.com/
    ```
    . On the homepage, you'll see a download button for your operating system (Windows, macOS,

or Linux). Choose the one that matches your computer and click **Download**.

2. **Install VS Code:**

   Once the download is complete, run the installer. Follow the setup instructions and make sure to check the box that says **Add to PATH** if prompted (just like with Python). After installation, open VS Code.

3. **Install the Python extension for VS Code:**

   To write Python code in VS Code, you need to install a Python extension. Open VS Code, and on the left-hand sidebar, click on the **Extensions** icon (it looks like four squares). In the search bar, type "Python" and install the first extension by Microsoft.

Writing Your First Program (Hello, World!)

Now that you have Python and VS Code all set up, it's time to write your very first program! Traditionally, the first program anyone writes when learning a new language is called "Hello, World!." It's a simple program that outputs the words "Hello, World!" on the screen. Although it's basic, this small victory is a major step in your coding journey.

Here's how to write and run your first Python program:

Step 1: Open VS Code

- Open **Visual Studio Code** on your computer.

- You should see a welcome screen. If it's not there, don't worry—you can always start by opening a new file.

Step 2: Create a New File

- Click **File** in the top-left corner of the window, then select **New File**.

- You will now have a blank space to write your code.

Step 3: Save the File

- Before you write any code, let's save the file. Go to **File > Save As**, and save the file with the name `hello.py`.

- **Note**: Make sure the file extension is `.py` (which stands for Python). This tells VS Code that the file contains Python code.

Step 4: Write the Code

Now for the fun part! Type the following line of code into the editor:

```
print("Hello, World!")
```

Step 5: Run the Program

Once you've written the code, it's time to run it. There are a few ways to do this in VS Code, but we'll use the easiest method:

- Right-click anywhere inside the code editor window.

- From the dropdown menu, select **Run Python File in Terminal**.

When you do this, the code will execute, and at the bottom of your VS Code window (in the **Terminal**), you'll see the output:

```
Hello, World!
```

Congratulations! You've just written and run your first Python program!

Breaking It Down: What Does This Code Do?

Let's take a moment to understand what this simple line of code is doing.

`print()`: This is a function in Python that tells the computer to display whatever is inside the parentheses. In this case, it's the phrase **"Hello, World!"**.

`"Hello, World!"`: This is the text that you want the computer to print. The quotation marks tell Python that this is a string (i.e., a sequence of characters), and not a variable or a number.

It's that simple! Every time you run this code, the computer will print "Hello, World!" on the screen. This tiny program may seem basic, but it's the first step in learning how to communicate with your computer.

What's Next?

You've just learned how to:

- Write your first program.

- Run it in VS Code.

- See the output in the terminal.

From here, we're going to gradually build on this foundation, exploring more complex concepts like **variables**, **data types**, and **control structures**. Don't worry, though—we'll take it slow, and before you know it, you'll be creating programs that do more than just say "Hello, World!"!

## Chapter 3

Breaking Down Problems: The Art of Logic

Welcome to the next chapter of your programming journey! Now that you've written your first program, it's time to focus on a core skill every programmer must master: **problem-solving**.

In programming, solving problems is what it's all about. But here's the secret: You don't have to be a genius or have superhuman logic skills to become great at it. You just need to learn how to break down problems into smaller pieces and solve each piece, one at a time.

Algorithmic Thinking for Everyday Problems

What is algorithmic thinking? It's a fancy term for something you already do every day—whether you realize it or not. Algorithmic thinking is the ability to think through problems logically and systematically.

Let's look at some real-world examples from everyday life where you're already practicing algorithmic thinking:

Example 1: Organizing a Family Function

Imagine you're planning a small family gathering, like a birthday party. You have a lot to consider:

- **Venue**: Where will the party be held?

- **Food**: What will you serve? Who will cater?

- **Guests**: Who's invited, and how will you send out invites?

- **Decorations**: Do you need to arrange for decorations?

Breaking this problem down involves answering each of these questions separately. Instead of panicking over everything at once, you focus on one part of the problem, like finalizing the guest list, before moving on to the next, such as organizing the food. That's algorithmic thinking in action!

Example 2: Navigating Through Traffic

Let's say you live in a city like Bengaluru or Delhi, and you're trying to navigate through heavy traffic. You have multiple routes to choose from, but which one will get you to your destination the fastest? You start by:

1. **Analyzing your options**: You can take the highway, back roads, or use public transport.

2. **Checking real-time traffic data**: Use an app like Google Maps to see which route has the least traffic.

3. **Making a decision**: Based on the data, you choose the route that will take the least time.

This process is no different from what you do in programming: break down the task, gather information, and make a decision based on the logic you've applied.

Example 3: Morning Routine

Think of something as simple as your daily morning routine. From waking up to leaving for work or college, you follow a set of steps in a particular order:

- Wake up.

- Brush your teeth.

- Take a shower.

- Get dressed.

- Have breakfast.

- Leave for work or school.

If you mix up these steps, your morning wouldn't go smoothly, right? Similarly, in programming, getting the sequence right is essential for solving problems correctly. Each step builds on the previous one, leading to the final result.

Step-by-Step Problem Solving

Now that we've seen how algorithmic thinking plays out in daily life, let's bring this skill into the world of programming. Here's how to approach problem-solving in code.

Step 1: Understand the Problem

The first step in solving any problem is to understand what exactly you're trying to do. Let's say you need to write a program that calculates how much money you'll save after a shopping discount.

- **Problem**: Calculate the final price after applying a discount to an item.

- **Input**: The original price of the item and the discount percentage.

- **Output**: The price after the discount has been applied.

Step 2: Break It Down

Once you understand the problem, break it down into smaller steps. For the shopping discount problem:

1. Ask the user for the original price of the item.

2. Ask for the discount percentage.

3. Calculate the discount amount.

4. Subtract the discount from the original price.

5. Display the final price to the user.

Step 3: Solve Each Piece

Now, tackle each step one by one. For example:

- **Step 1**: Ask the user for input. In Python, you'll use the `input()` function to get the original price and discount from the user.

- **Step 2**: Convert the input into numbers. By default Python doesn't know if the input is number or text.

- **Step 3**: Calculate the discount by multiplying the price by the percentage.

- **Step 4**: Subtract the discount from the original price.

- **Step 5**: Print the final price.

Here's how the code might look:

```python
# Step 1: Ask for input
original_price = float(input("Enter the original price: "))
    discount_percentage = float(input("Enter the discount percentage: "))

    # Step 2: Calculate the discount
    discount_amount = (discount_percentage / 100) * original_price

    # Step 3: Subtract the discount from the original price
    final_price = original_price - discount_amount

    # Step 4: Display the final price
    print(f"The final price after the discount is: ₹{final_price}")
```

Explanation:

- `input()`: This function takes input from the user as a string.

- `float()`: Converts the string input into a decimal number.

- `print()`: Outputs the result to the screen.

- `f` **in** `print()`: This is part of a feature in Python called **f-strings** (formatted string literals). The `f` before the string allows us to embed variables directly into the string. For example, inside the curly braces `{final_price}`, Python automatically inserts the value of the `final_price` variable into the string.

Instead of writing something like:

```
print("The final price after the
discount is: ₹" + str(final_price))
```

which can get complicated, f-strings make it much cleaner and easier to read. We'll dive deeper into strings and f-strings in an upcoming chapter!Notice how we broke the problem down and solved each piece individually. This process makes it easier to tackle even complex problems.

Step 4: Test and Tweak

In programming, it's normal for things not to work perfectly on the first try. Maybe your program doesn't handle decimal points correctly, or it throws an error when the user enters invalid input. That's okay!

Once you've written the code, test it with different inputs. If something doesn't work, go back, tweak the code, and try again. Problem-solving is an iterative process, and every attempt gets you closer to the solution.

Putting It All Together: Coding in Real Life

Coding isn't just about learning syntax or memorizing commands—it's about learning to think differently. By learning to break down problems and solve them step by step, you'll develop skills that apply not only to programming but to real-life challenges as well.

Whether you're organizing a family event, navigating traffic, or handling daily tasks, you're already using algorithmic thinking. Now, with the power of code, you can take this logical problem-solving to a whole new level.

Chapter 4

Variables and Data Types

Welcome to one of the most exciting parts of coding—**variables and data types**! You can think of variables as little containers that hold information for you. And the type of information they hold? Well, that's where data types come in.

What Are Variables?

Imagine you have a piggy bank at home. Every time you put money into it, you're storing something valuable. But what happens when you want to count how much money is inside? You can't know unless you store that information somewhere in your mind or on paper. Variables in programming are like your piggy bank—except instead of coins, they hold numbers, text, or even whole lists of things!

Here's how we create a variable in Python:

```
age = 20

name = "Amit"

is_student = True
```

In this code:

- `age` is a variable that stores the number `20`.

- `name` is a variable that stores the text (called a string) **"Amit"**.

- `is_student` is a variable that stores the value `True`, which is a **boolean** (a fancy way of saying "true or false").

Variables are important because they allow us to reuse and change values as our program runs.

Numbers, Text, and Truths: Basic Data Types

In Python (and most programming languages), there are different types of data that variables can hold. Here are the most common ones you'll encounter:

1. **Integers**: These are whole numbers, like 5, 100, or -42.

   Example:

   ```
   number_of_students = 50
   ```

2. **Floats**: These are decimal numbers, like 3.14, 99.99, or -0.01.

   Example:

   ```
   price_of_milk = 30.5
   ```

3. **Strings**: These are sequences of characters, like words or sentences. Strings are always enclosed in quotes.

   Example:

   ```
   favorite_color = "blue"
   ```

4. **Booleans**: These represent True or False values, which are often used in decision-making.

Example:

```python
is_raining = False
```

Working with Numbers in Python

Let's say you're buying groceries at your neighborhood market. You know that a kilogram of rice costs ₹60, and you want to buy 5 kg. You can use variables to help you figure out the total cost:

```python
price_per_kg = 60
quantity = 5
total_cost = price_per_kg * quantity
print(f"The total cost is ₹{total_cost}")
```

Here's what's happening:

- We store the price of rice in a variable called `price_per_kg`.
- We store the quantity of rice in a variable called `quantity`.

- Then, we calculate the `total_cost` by multiplying the two values, and use **f-strings** to print the result.

Chapter 5

Operators: Doing Math with Code

Welcome to Chapter 5! By now, you've got a solid foundation of variables and data types, so you're ready to make your programs do a bit more. This chapter is all about operators, the tools that allow your code to perform calculations, compare values, and even make decisions. In other words, operators are the workhorses of programming—they help you manipulate data and make your programs more dynamic.

Think of operators like the tools in your kitchen: a knife to cut, a spoon to stir, and a stove to cook. Similarly, operators help you "work" with data. Whether you're adding numbers, comparing values, or checking conditions, operators make it all possible.

Arithmetic Operators: Let's Do Some Math!

Arithmetic operators are the ones that help you do math in your code. These are super straightforward—you've been using them all your life in basic math classes. Here are the most common arithmetic operators in Python:

Operator	Description	Example
+	Addition	5 + 3 → 8
-	Subtraction	5 - 3 → 2
*	Multiplication	5 * 3 → 15
/	Division	5 / 2 → 2.5
//	Floor Division	5 // 2 → 2
%	Modulus (Remainder)	5 % 2 → 1
**	Exponentiation	5 ** 2 → 25

Addition (+)

The addition operator + does exactly what you'd expect—it adds two numbers together.

```
a = 5
b = 10
print(a + b)
```

Output:

```
15
```

Subtraction (-)

The subtraction operator - subtracts one number from another.

```
a = 15
b = 5
print(a - b)
```

Output:

```
10
```

Multiplication (*)

The multiplication operator * multiplies two numbers together.

```
a = 6
b = 4
print(a * b)
```

Output:

```
24
```

Division (/)

The division operator / divides one number by another. The result will always be a floating-point number (i.e., a decimal).

```
a = 20
b = 4
print(a / b)
```

Output:

```
5.0
```

Even if the result is a whole number, Python gives the answer in floating-point form. In this case, **5.0**.

Floor Division (//)

Now, if you want the result of the division to be a whole number, you can use floor division (//), which ignores the decimal part and gives the "floor" value.

```
a = 20
b = 3
print(a // b)
```

Output:

```
6
```

Here, the exact result is **6.666...**, but floor division gives you just **6**.

Modulus (%)

The modulus operator **%** gives you the remainder of a division. It's useful when you need to check if a number is divisible by another number.

```
a = 10
b = 3
print(a % b)
```

Output:

```
1
```

Here, 10 divided by 3 gives a remainder of 1. This operator is particularly useful for tasks like checking whether a number is odd or even.

Exponentiation (**)

The exponentiation operator ** raises a number to the power of another number.

```
a = 2
b = 3
print(a ** b)
```

Output:

```
8
```

In this case, 2 ** 3 means "2 raised to the power of 3," which is 2 * 2 * 2 = 8.

Comparison Operators: Evaluating Relationships

Comparison operators help you compare two values. These comparisons result in a Boolean value—either True or False. Let's go over the most common comparison operators.

Operator	Description	Example
==	Equal to	5 == 5 → True
!=	Not equal to	5 != 3 → True
>	Greater than	5 > 3 → True
<	Less than	5 < 3 → False
>=	Greater than or equal to	5 >= 5 → True
<=	Less than or equal to	5 <= 3 → False

Equal to (==)

The == operator checks if two values are equal.

```python
a = 5
b = 5
print(a == b)
```

Output:

```
True
```

Not equal to (!=)

The != operator checks if two values are not equal.

```python
a = 5
b = 5
print(a != b)
```

Output:

```
False
```

Greater than (>)

The > operator checks if one value is greater than another.

```
a = 10
b = 5
print(a > b)
```

Output:

```
True
```

Less than (<)

The < operator checks if one value is less than another.

```
a = 3
b = 10
print(a < b)
```

Output:

```
True
```

Greater than or equal to >=)

The `>=` operator checks if one value is greater than or equal to another.

```
a = 10
b = 10
print(a >= b)
```

Output:

```
True
```

Less than or equal to (<=)

The `<=` operator checks if one value is less than or equal to another.

```
a = 3
b = 5
print(a <= b)
```

Output:

```
True
```

Logical Operators: Combining Conditions

Logical operators are used to combine multiple conditions. They allow your program to make more complex decisions.

Operator	Description	Example
and	True if both are true	True and False — False
or	True if at least one is true	True or False — True
not	Inverts the truth value	not True — False

and

The **and** operator ensures that **both** conditions are true for the entire expression to be true.

```
a = 5
b = 10
print(a < 10 and b > 5)
```

Output:

```
True
```

Here, both `a < 10` and `b > 5` are true, so the result is `True`.

or

The or operator ensures that at least one condition is true for the expression to be true.

```
a = 5
b = 3
print(a > 10 or b < 5)
```

Output:

```
True
```

In this case, a > 10 is false, but b < 5 is true, so the result is True because or only needs one condition to be true.

not

The **not** operator inverts the value of a Boolean expression. If the condition is true, **not** makes it false, and vice versa.

```
a = 5
b = 3
print(not a > b)
```

Output:

```
False
```

Here, **a > 5** is true, but **not** makes it false.

Assignment Operators: Simplifying Assignments

Assignment operators are used to assign values to variables, often in a more concise way.

Operator	Description	Example
=	Assign	x = 5
+=	Add and assign	x += 2 (same as x = x + 2)
-=	Subtract and assign	x -= 1 (same as x = x - 1)
*=	Multiply and assign	x *= 3 (same as x = x * 3)
/=	Divide and assign	x /= 2 (same as x = x / 2)

Here is a simple example to give you a basic idea of how assignment operators work. Let's put **+=** operator into play:

```
score = 5
score += 10
print(f'Score: {score}')
```

Output:

```
Score: 15
```

Final Thoughts

Now that you've learned about operators, you can perform all sorts of calculations and make decisions in your code. Operators are essential in programming, just like how spices are essential in cooking a delicious meal!

Control Structures: If, Else, and More

Welcome to Chapter 6! So far, we've covered a lot of the basics—variables, data types, and operators—but now, we'll take things up a notch. What if we want our program to make decisions based on certain conditions? This is where control structures come in.

Control structures allow us to control the flow of a program. They help the program decide what to do next based on conditions. You can think of them as traffic signals for your code. Just like how traffic lights control when you stop, go, or wait, control structures decide when certain parts of your code should run.

Making Decisions in Code

Have you ever asked yourself, "Should I go out for tea or coffee?" The decision depends on a condition—like what you feel like drinking at that moment. Similarly, in programming, we use control structures to decide which block of code should be executed based on conditions.

In Python, we have a few key control structures: `if`, `else`, and `elif` (short for "else if").

`if` Statements: The Basics

The `if` statement is the most basic form of decision-making in programming. If a condition is true, the code inside the if block will run. If it's false, the code will be skipped.

Syntax:

```
if condition:
    # Code to execute if the
    condition is true
```

Let's break this down with an example.

Example: Deciding What to Wear

Imagine you're deciding what to wear based on the weather. If it's raining, you'll wear a raincoat.

```python
is_raining = True
if is_raining:
    print("Don't forget your raincoat!")
```

Output:

```
Don't forget your raincoat!
```

If the condition (`is_raining == True`) is met, the program prints the message. If the condition was false, the program would skip the `print` statement.

Conditional Statements: Adding Flexibility

What if you want the program to do one thing if a condition is true and something else if it's false? That's where the `else` statement comes in.

`else` Statements: The Backup Plan

The else statement runs when the if condition is false. Think of it as a backup plan.

Syntax:

```python
if condition:
    # Code to execute if
    condition is true
else:
    # Code to execute if
    condition is false
```

Example: Making Tea or Coffee

Let's say you can't decide between tea or coffee. If there's tea available, you'll make tea, but if there's no tea, you'll go for coffee.

```python
tea_available = False

if tea_available:
    print("Making a cup of tea.")
else:
    print("Making a cup of coffee.")
```

Output:

```
Making a cup of coffee.
```

In this case, since tea is not available (`tea_available == False`), the program defaults to making coffee. Pretty neat, right?

`elif` Statements: More Than Two Options

What if you have more than two choices? Enter the `elif` statement! This is short for "else if," and it allows you to add multiple conditions to your **if-else** block.

Syntax:

```python
if condition1:
    # Code to execute if condition1
    is true
elif condition2:
    # Code to execute if condition2
    is true
else:
    # Code to execute if none of the
    above conditions are true
```

Example: Choosing a Mode of Transport

Let's say you're trying to decide how to get to work. If you have a bike, you'll ride it. If not, but there's a bus, you'll take the bus. If neither is available, you'll walk.

```python
bike_available = False

bus_available = True

if bike_available:
    print("Riding the bike to
    work.")
elif bus_available:
    print("Taking the bus to work.")
else:
    print("Walking to work.")
```

Output

```
Taking the bus to work.
```

Here, since no bike is available but the bus is, the program prints the message for taking the bus. If neither option was available, it would print that you're walking to work.

Example: Traffic Signals

Here's an everyday scenario from roads that can be related to decision-making in code. Think about traffic signals:

- If the light is green, you go.

- If the light is yellow, you slow down.

- If the light is red, you stop.

This could be easily translated into a Python program using **if**, **elif**, and **else**:

```python
traffic_light = "red"

if traffic_light == "green":
    print("Go!")
elif traffic_light == "yellow":
    print("Slow down.")
else:
    print("Stop.")
```

Output:

```
    Stop.
```

Nested `if` Statements: Conditions Within Conditions

You can even nest **if** statements inside other **if** statements. This is useful when you need more detailed checks.

```python
is_member = True
is_birthday = True

if is_member:
    if is_birthday:
        print("You get a 20% discount!")
    else:
        print("You get a 10% discount!")
else:
    print("Sorry, no discount.")
```

Example: Checking for Discounts

Imagine you're shopping online. You get a discount if you're a member, and a bigger discount if it's your birthday.

Output:

```
You get a 20% discount!
```

Boolean Expressions: The Heart of Conditional Logic

The conditions in an **if** statement are evaluated as Boolean expressions. A Boolean expression is just a fancy way of saying that the expression can either be **True** or **False**.

For instance, **5 > 3** is a Boolean expression, and it evaluates to **True**. Similarly, **5 < 3** evaluates to **False.**

Combining Conditions with Logical Operators

Sometimes you need to check more than one condition at a time. This is where logical operators like **and, or,** and **not** come into play.

- **and:** Both conditions must be true.

- **or:** At least one condition must be true.

- **not:** Inverts the condition.

Example: Getting a Ride

Let's say you'll get a ride to the market if either your cousin or your sibling is available. You can check that using the or operator:

```python
cousin_available = False
sibling_available = True


if cousin_available or sibling_available:
    print("You have a ride to the market!")
else:
    print("You need to walk to the market.")
```

Output:

```
You have a ride to the market!
```

Since at least one of the two is available, the program prints that you have a ride.

Writing Clean and Readable Code

One thing to remember while using control structures is to keep your code **readable**. Just like how you wouldn't give someone a messy room to live in, you don't want your code to be messy and hard to read.

Here are some tips:

- **Indentation**: Python relies on indentation (spaces or tabs) to define blocks of code. Make sure each level of decision-making (like inside an `if` or `else` block) is indented properly.

- **Comments**: Add comments to explain what your code is doing. This is especially helpful when you come back to the code later or when someone else is reading your code.

```python
# Checking if the traffic light is
green, yellow, or red
traffic_light = "green"
if traffic_light == "green":
    print("Go!")
elif traffic_light == "yellow":
    print("Prepare to stop.")
else:
    print("Stop!")
```

Example: Ice Cream Decision

Let's end this chapter with a fun example. Imagine you're walking by your favorite ice cream shop. You love ice cream, but you're trying to eat healthy.

Here's how you can decide:

- If it's a hot day and your favorite flavor is available, you'll buy ice cream.

- If it's hot but your flavor isn't available, you'll have lemonade instead.

- If it's not a hot day, you'll skip the treat.

Let's turn that into Python code:

```python
hot_day = True
favorite_flavor_available = False
if hot_day:
    if favorite_flavor_available:
        print("Yay! I'll have my
        favorite ice cream.")
    else:
        print("It's hot, but no
        favorite flavor. I'll have
        lemonade.")
else:
    print("It's not hot, so I'll skip
    the treat.")
```

Output:

```
It's hot, but no favorite
flavor. I'll have lemonade.
```

This nested **if** example shows how you can combine multiple conditions to make decisions—just like in real life.

Conclusion

Control structures like **if**, **else**, and **elif** are the heart of decision-making in programming. They allow your program to respond differently to different situations, just like we do in our daily lives. Whether it's deciding when to cross the street at a traffic signal or picking what to eat based on the time of day, Python's control structures help bring logic to your code.

## Chapter 7

Loops: Repeating Tasks with Ease

Ever feel like you're doing the same thing over and over again? Like hitting the snooze button on your alarm or checking your phone repeatedly to see if a message has arrived? That's what loops are for in programming! They help you automate repetitive tasks so you don't have to keep writing the same code again and again.

Imagine telling someone to fold 100 clothes manually without using any shortcut. It would be tedious, right? In the world of code, **loops** are like that magical shortcut that helps you repeat tasks without getting tired. You can tell the program, "Keep doing this until I say stop!"

In Python, there are two types of loops:

- **For loops** - Used when you know how many times you want to repeat a task.

- **While loops** - Used when you want to repeat a task until a certain condition is met.

Introduction to Loops

Loops allow you to repeat a block of code as many times as you want. Let's say you want to print "Good morning" five times—writing the `print()` statement five times would be tedious. Instead, you can use a loop to handle this repetition for you.

Example: Drinking 8 Glasses of Water

Let's start with a simple daily example. Imagine your doctor advised you to drink 8 glasses of water every day to stay hydrated. Instead of repeating the task manually every hour, you could set up a loop in your head: Drink one glass every hour until you reach 8 glasses.

In Python, it would look like this using a **for** loop:

```python
for glass in range(1, 9):
    print(f"Drink glass number
    {glass}")
```

Output:

```
Drink glass number 1
Drink glass number 2
Drink glass number 3
Drink glass number 4
Drink glass number 5
Drink glass number 6
Drink glass number 7
Drink glass number 8
```

In this code, we use the **range()** function to loop from 1 to 8. For each glass of water, the program prints a message reminding you to drink it.

`for` Loops: When You Know How Many Times

A `for` loop is used when you know how many times you want to repeat something. Let's say you want to hand out 100 sweets to kids at a birthday party. Instead of handing out sweets one by one manually in the code, you can use a `for` loop to automate this task.

```python
for sweet in range(1, 101):
    print(f"Handing out sweet
    number {sweet}")
```

Output:

```
Handing out sweet number 1
Handing out sweet number 2
...
Handing out sweet number 100
```

This is how simple it is to perform repetitive tasks using a `for` loop!

`while` Loops: When You Don't Know When to Stop

A `while` loop is used when you want to keep repeating a task until a specific condition is met. Unlike a `for` loop, you may not know how many times the task will repeat—this loop will keep running until the condition becomes false.

Example: Waiting for an Auto-Rickshaw

Imagine you're standing on the roadside waiting for an auto-rickshaw. You don't know how many auto-rickshaws will pass before you find one that's available. You'll keep looking until one finally stops for you. In Python, this scenario can be represented by a `while` loop:

```python
rickshaw_available = False
tries = 0
while not rickshaw_available:
    tries += 1
    print(f"Checking auto-rickshaw, attempt {tries}")

    if tries == 5:  # Let's assume the 5th rickshaw is available
        rickshaw_available = True
        print("Auto-rickshaw found!")
```

Output:

```
Checking auto-rickshaw, attempt 1
Checking auto-rickshaw, attempt 2
Checking auto-rickshaw, attempt 3
Checking auto-rickshaw, attempt 4
Checking auto-rickshaw, attempt 5
Auto-rickshaw found!
```

Here, the loop keeps running, checking for an available rickshaw until we find one. After 5 tries, we get one, and the loop stops.

Example: Filling Water Balloons

Here's another fun example. Let's say you're filling water balloons for Holi. You want to fill 10 balloons, but you need to check if the balloon is strong enough to hold the water each time.

This is where a `while` loop can help. Imagine you fill one balloon, test its strength, and only then move on to the next balloon.

```python
filled_balloons = 0
strong_balloon = True

while filled_balloons < 10:
    print(f"Filling balloon number
    {filled_balloons + 1}")

    if strong_balloon:
        filled_balloons += 1   # Add
        1 to filled_balloons if
        balloon is strong
    else:
        print("This balloon popped.
        Trying again.")
```

Output:

```
Filling balloon number 1
Filling balloon number 2

...

Filling balloon number 10
```

In this case, the loop repeats until 10 strong balloons are filled.

Breaking Out of Loops: When You Want to Stop Early

Sometimes, you might want to stop a loop early—like when you find what you're looking for before reaching the end of the loop. This is done using the **break** statement.

Example: Searching for a Book in the Library

Imagine you're looking for a specific book in a library. You don't know exactly where it is, but you'll keep searching through the shelves until you find it. Once you find it, you can stop searching.

Let's simulate that in Python:

```python
shelves = ["Math", "History",
"Programming", "Physics"]
book_to_find = "Programming"
for shelf in shelves:
    print(f"Searching in the {shelf}
    section")
    if shelf == book_to_find:
        print(f"Found the {book_to_
        find} book!")
        break
```

Output:

```
Searching in the Math section
Searching in the History section
Searching in the Programming section
Found the Programming book!
```

Here, once the book is found in the "Programming" section, the loop stops, and the program doesn't search further.

Continue: Skipping a Step in a Loop

You can also use the continue statement to skip the current iteration of a loop and move on to the next one. It's like saying, "I'm done with this step; let's move on."

Example: Skipping Ads in a YouTube Playlist

Imagine you're watching a playlist of videos on YouTube. Every time an ad comes up, you skip it and go directly to the video. You don't want to stop watching the whole playlist; you just want to skip the ads.

Here's how you can do that in Python:

```
videos = ["video", "ad",
"video", "video", "ad"]
for item in videos:
    if item == "ad":
        print("Skipping ad...")
        continue
    print("Watching", item)
```

Output:

```
Watching video
Skipping ad...
Watching video
Watching video
Skipping ad...
```

Whenever the program encounters an "ad," it skips it and continues with the next item in the list.

A Looping Example: Organizing Festival Celebrations

Let's imagine you're organizing Diwali celebrations in your neighborhood. You need to distribute sweets to every family in the locality, one at a time. You can automate this task with a loop that repeats the process for every family.

```python
families = ["Sharma", "Gupta", "Verma", "Khan", "Patel"]

for family in families:
    print(f"Delivering sweets to the {family} family")
```

Output:

```
Delivering sweets to the Sharma family
Delivering sweets to the Gupta family
Delivering sweets to the Verma family
Delivering sweets to the Khan family
Delivering sweets to the Patel family
```

Now, you might be wondering what the list of families `["Sharma", "Gupta", "Verma", "Khan", "Patel"])` is. Don't worry—this is what we call an **array** (or a **list** in Python). You don't need to fully understand arrays just yet! Later in the book, we'll dive deep into arrays and show you how to work with them effectively. For now, just think of it as a simple way to store multiple items in one place, like a grocery list!

Conclusion

Loops are incredibly powerful tools that let you repeat tasks without writing the same code over and over. Whether you're handing out sweets at a party, filling balloons for a celebration, or searching for books in a library, loops allow you to simplify repetitive tasks and make your code more efficient.

In this chapter, we learned about:

- **For loops**: Used when you know how many times to repeat a task.

- **While loops**: Used when you want to repeat a task until a condition is met.

- **Break and continue**: Handy tools to control when a loop stops or skips steps.

In the next chapter, we'll dive into **functions**, which allow you to group together blocks of code and use them again and again. Get ready to take your coding skills to the next level!

## Chapter 8

Functions: Building Blocks of Code

Imagine this: You're in the kitchen, ready to prepare your favorite drink—Masala Chai. Now, making chai is something you've done countless times, and it's pretty straightforward. You boil water, add tea leaves, throw in spices, simmer milk, and voila—delicious chai is ready. But what if every time someone asked for chai, you had to explain or repeat every single step? Wouldn't it be easier if you could just write down the recipe once and reuse it?

That's exactly what a **function** does in programming.

What Are Functions?

Functions allow you to bundle a set of instructions together, give it a name, and then reuse those instructions whenever you need them. Instead of writing the same block of code over and over again, you just "call" the function, and it takes care of the task.

In simple terms, a function is like a recipe—you give it ingredients (called **arguments**) and it returns something delicious (called a **return value**).

Let's see an example of how functions work, starting with a classic chai recipe.

Defining a Function: Making Masala Chai

Here's how you'd define a function to make masala chai in code:

```python
def make_masala_chai():
    water = 1  # in cups
    tea_leaves = 2  # teaspoons
    sugar = 2  # teaspoons
    milk = 1  # in cups
    spices = ["ginger", "cardamom"]

    print(f"Boil {water} cup of
water.")
    print(f"Add {tea_leaves}
teaspoons of tea leaves.")
    print(f"Add {sugar} teaspoons of
sugar.")
    print(f"Simmer with {milk}
cup of milk and spices: {',
'.join(spices)}.")
    print("Your masala chai is
ready!")
```

You've just defined a function called **make_masala_chai()** that prints out the steps to make chai. You can now reuse this function whenever you want!

Calling a Function: Ask for Chai Anytime!

Now, whenever someone asks you for chai, you can just call the function:

```
make_masala_chai()
```

Output:

```
Boil 1 cup of water.
    Add 2 teaspoons of tea leaves.
    Add 2 teaspoons of sugar.
    Simmer with 1 cup of milk and
    spices: ginger, cardamom.
    Your masala chai is ready!
```

See how easy that was? Instead of writing all the steps over and over again, you simply call the function. In the same way, functions make your programming life easier.

Why Use Functions?

Here's why functions are so powerful:

- **Reusability**: You can reuse functions without rewriting code.

- **Modularity**: Functions make your code more organized and easier to read.

- **Abstraction**: When you use a function, you don't need to worry about the details—just like you don't need to think about all the steps to make chai each time.

Example: Ordering Your Favorite Food

Let's say you've developed a habit of ordering your favorite food—say, paneer butter masala—every Friday from the same restaurant. You could call up the restaurant and repeat the same order each week, but it would be much easier to just store that order as a function and reuse it every time.

Here's how that would look in code:

```python
def order_food():
    food = "Paneer Butter Masala"
    quantity = 2
    print(f"Ordering {quantity}
    plates of {food}.")
```

You can now call order_food() every Friday and it'll order your favorite dish without you having to type it out every time!

Function Arguments: Customizing the Recipe

But what if your friend wants to order something different? In that case, we can use arguments to customize the order. Let's rewrite the **order_food** function to take a food item and quantity as arguments:

```python
def order_food(food, quantity):
    print(f"Ordering {quantity}
    plates of {food}.")
```

Now, you can place custom orders:

```python
order_food("Chole Bhature", 3)
order_food("Dosa", 2)
```

Output:

```
Ordering 3 plates of Chole
Bhature.
    Ordering 2 plates of Dosa.
```

By passing in arguments, you can now order any food in any quantity—just like modifying a recipe for different tastes.

Returning Values: Bringing Home the Food

Functions not only perform tasks, they can also return something back to you. Think of it as going to a restaurant, ordering food, and then receiving the food back to enjoy.

For example, let's create a function that returns the total price of your order:

```python
def calculate_total(quantity,
price_per_item):
    total = quantity * price_per_
item
    return total
```

Now, when you call the function:

```python
total_price = calculate_total(3,
150)
    print(f"Total price is:
    ₹{total_price}")
```

Output:

```
         Total price is: ₹450
```

Here, the function `calculate_total()` does the math for you and returns the total cost.

Putting It All Together: Building Your Own Functions

Think of functions as tools you can customize, like a Swiss Army knife. You'll define many functions as you continue your coding journey, and each one will help you break down complex problems into manageable pieces.

Final Thought: Function Like a Pro

Learning to use functions is a game-changer. Whether you're making chai, ordering food, or solving a coding problem, functions simplify everything. They let you focus on the bigger picture, freeing your mind from repetitive tasks.

So next time you're asked to do something repetitive, whether it's in code or in real life, think: "Can I turn this into a function?"

And now that you know the basics of functions, you're well on your way to coding like a pro!

## Chapter 9

Lists and Dictionaries: Storing Data

In the world of programming, just like in real life, we often need a way to organize and manage multiple items. Think about it: When you go grocery shopping, do you remember each item by heart, or do you make a list? Or maybe you have a contact list on your phone to store names and phone numbers.

In Python, the tools we use for this kind of organization are called **lists** and **dictionaries**.

Introduction to Lists

Imagine you're heading to your local market to buy groceries. You might jot down something like this:

- Rice
- Daal
- Potatoes
- Milk
- Eggs

This is a **list**—a collection of items stored in a specific order. In Python, lists work exactly the same way.

Creating a List in Python

Here's how you can create a grocery list in Python:

```python
grocery_list = ["Rice", "Daal", "Potatoes", "Milk", "Eggs"]
print(grocery_list)
```

Output:

```
['Rice', 'Daal', 'Potatoes',
'Milk', 'Eggs']
```

Just like that, you have a list of items stored in one place. You can add, remove, or modify items in your list, making it super flexible.

Accessing Items in a List

Let's say you want to check what the second item on your grocery list is. You can do that easily by using the **index** of the item (remember, Python uses zero-based indexing):

```
print(grocery_list[1])
```

Output:

```
Daal
```

In this case, **grocery_list[1]** gives you the second item, which is "Daal". Easy, right?

Modifying a List

What if you decide to buy tea leaves instead of milk? You can update your list like this:

```
grocery_list[3] = "Tea Leaves"
print(grocery_list)
```

Output:

```
['Rice', 'Daal', 'Potatoes',
'Tea Leaves', 'Eggs']
```

Now you've swapped out milk for tea leaves. Lists let you change or add items as needed, just like you'd do with a physical shopping list.

Example: Packing for a Trip

Let's move beyond groceries. Imagine you're packing for a family road trip to Goa. You might have a list of essentials like this:

```
packing_list = ["Sunscreen",
"Sunglasses", "Clothes", "Snacks",
"Charger"]
```

This list helps you stay organized. If you realize you forgot to add something—say, a hat—you can add it later:

```
packing_list.append("Hat")
print(packing_list)
```

Output:

```
['Sunscreen', 'Sunglasses',
'Clothes', 'Snacks',
'Charger', 'Hat']
```

Lists Are Great, But What If...?

Lists are great when you just need a collection of items. But what if you need more information? For example, what if you want to store both the **name** and **phone**

number of a contact in your phone? This is where **dictionaries** come in.

Introduction to Dictionaries: Storing Key-Value Pairs

Think of a **dictionary** like your phone's contact list. For each contact, you store a **name** (the key) and a **phone number** (the value). In a dictionary, each key is associated with a specific value.

Here's how you can create a dictionary in Python:

```python
contacts = {
    "Ravi": "9876543210",
    "Priya": "9123456789",
    "Amit": "9988776655"
    }
```

Now, you have a dictionary of contacts where each person's name is linked to their phone number.

Accessing Data in a Dictionary

Want to know Amit's phone number? You can access it like this:

```
print(contacts["Amit"])
```

Output:

```
9988776655
```

By using the key ("Amit"), you can get the associated value ("9988776655").

Modifying Data in a Dictionary

What if Amit changes his number? You can update his contact information like this:

```
contacts["Amit"] = "9911223344"
print(contacts)
```

Output:

```
{'Ravi': '9876543210',
'Priya': '9123456789', 'Amit':
'9911223344'}
```

Dictionaries allow you to modify data easily by changing the value associated with a key.

Example: Organizing Your Family's Favorite Dishes

Let's say you want to keep track of your family's favorite dishes. You could create a dictionary like this:

```python
favorite_dishes = {
    "Dad": "Rajma Chawal",
    "Mom": "Dosa",
    "Sister": "Paneer Tikka",
    "You": "Pav Bhaji"
    }
```

Now, whenever you're wondering what to cook for dinner, you can simply check the dictionary:

```python
print(favorite_dishes["Dad"])
```

Output:

```
Rajma Chawal
```

Combining Lists and Dictionaries

Here's where things get fun. You can use lists and dictionaries together to create more complex data structures.

For example, let's say you want to create a menu for your next party. Each dish will have its name and a list of ingredients:

```python
menu = {
    "Chole Bhature": ["Chickpeas",
    "Flour", "Onions", "Tomatoes",
    "Spices"],

    "Biryani": ["Rice", "Chicken",
    "Yogurt", "Spices"],

    "Gulab Jamun": ["Milk Solids",
    "Flour", "Sugar"]

}
```

Now, you can access the ingredients for any dish like this:

```python
print(menu["Biryani"])
```

Output:

```
['Rice', 'Chicken', 'Yogurt',
 'Spices']
```

This is how lists and dictionaries allow you to organize complex sets of data in a simple, structured way.

Conclusion: Organizing Like a Pro

Whether you're creating a grocery list, storing contacts, or keeping track of your favorite recipes, **lists** and **dictionaries** help you organize data efficiently. In programming, they're your go-to tools for keeping things in order and easy to access.

With lists and dictionaries, you're already thinking like a programmer—structuring data in a way that's easy to manage and reuse. In the next chapter, we'll dive into **Error Handling**, where you'll learn how to deal with unexpected bumps in the road (because, let's be honest, life doesn't always go as planned).

## Chapter 10

Error Handling

Mistakes happen. Whether you're burning your toast or locking yourself out of the house, life is full of little errors. In programming, errors are just as common, and learning how to handle them is an essential part of becoming a skilled coder. Thankfully, Python provides tools to deal with these issues without letting them bring your whole program crashing down.

In this chapter, we'll explore how to handle errors in Python using **try-except blocks**. This will allow you to catch and manage problems, just like how your mom knows exactly what to do when the pressure cooker whistles a little too early!

What Happens When Code Breaks?

Before we dive into error handling, let's understand what happens when Python encounters an error. When something goes wrong in your code, Python raises an "exception." This is basically Python's way of saying, "Uh-oh, something's not right here!" If the exception isn't handled, the program will crash.

Let's look at an example:

```
number = int(input("Enter a
number: "))
    print("Your number is:",
number)
```

If you enter something that isn't a number, like "five", Python will throw a **ValueError** and stop the program. But we can prevent this from happening by handling the error.

Types of Errors in Python

There are several types of errors (also called **exceptions**) in Python:

- **SyntaxError**: This happens when the code is written incorrectly, such as forgetting a colon or a closing bracket.

- **ValueError**: This occurs when you pass an argument of the right type, but the value is inappropriate, like entering text when a number is expected.

- **IndexError**: Happens when you try to access an item in a list that doesn't exist. For example, trying to grab the 5th item from a list with only 3 items.

- **ZeroDivisionError**: Occurs when you try to divide a number by zero (which is a no-no in programming and math).

Handling Errors with Try-Except Blocks

Just like how you check if the gas is off before leaving the house, you can plan ahead in coding by using **try-except blocks**. These allow you to "try" a piece of code, and if an error occurs, the program will "catch" it and handle it smoothly.

Here's a simple example:

```
try:
    number = int(input("Enter a
    number: "))
    print("Your number is:", number)
except ValueError:
    print("Oops! That wasn't a
    valid number. Please try
    again.")
```

In this code, if the user enters something other than a number, the program won't crash. Instead, it will show a friendly message and continue running.

Example: Online Payment Failures

Let's say you're shopping online and trying to make a payment. You enter your card details, but you accidentally miss one digit. Instead of the website crashing, you get a message saying "Please enter a valid card number." That's error handling at work!

Here's how it would look in code:

```python
try:
    card_number = input("Enter your
card number: ")
    if len(card_number) != 16:
        raise ValueError("Invalid
        card number length")
    print("Payment processing...")
except ValueError as e:
    print(f"Error: {e}")
```

In this example, if the user enters a card number that isn't 16 digits long, the program throws an error but handles it gracefully by showing a message.

A Familiar Example: Cooking Gone Wrong

Imagine you're cooking chai, and you mistakenly add way too much sugar. You don't throw out the whole pot, right? Instead, you try to fix it by adding more water or milk. This is error handling in action. You catch the mistake (too much sugar), and you handle it (add water to balance).

Let's translate this into code:

```python
def make_chai(sugar_spoons):
    try:
        if sugar_spoons > 3:
            raise ValueError("Too
            much sugar!")
        print("Making chai with",
        sugar_spoons, "spoons of
        sugar.")
    except ValueError as e:
        print(f"Error: {e}. Adding
        more water to balance!")
```

Here, if you try to make chai with more than 3 spoons of sugar, the program throws an error, but it also knows how to handle it—by suggesting a fix!

Finally: Cleaning Up

Just like how you tidy up the kitchen after a cooking disaster, Python also allows you to clean up after handling errors, whether they occurred or not. This is done using the **finally** block. The **finally** block always runs, no matter what happens in the **try** or **except** blocks.

For example, let's say you're trying to open a file and read from it, but you always need to close the file at the end, no matter what:

```python
try:
    file = open("example.txt", "r")
    data = file.read()
except FileNotFoundError:
    print("File not found!")
finally:
    file.close()
    print("File closed.")
```

Even if the file isn't found, the**finally** block ensures that the file is closed properly. It's like cleaning up after trying out a recipe—whether it's a success or a flop, you still have to wash the dishes!

Nested Try-Except Blocks: Layering Your Safety Nets

Sometimes, you might need to handle multiple possible errors. Imagine you're on a road trip, and you first check if your car has enough fuel, then you check if your GPS is working. If either goes wrong, you handle the situation accordingly.

In code, it might look like this:

```python
try:
    distance = int(input("Enter
    the distance to your
    destination: "))
    fuel = int(input("Enter the
    amount of fuel left in your
    tank: "))
    if distance > fuel * 10:
        raise ValueError("Not
        enough fuel to reach the
        destination!")
    print("You're good to go!")
except ValueError as e:
    print(f"Error: {e}")
```

If the fuel isn't enough, the program raises an error, and you get a clear message that something is wrong.

Why Error Handling Matters

Without proper error handling, even small issues can cause your program to crash. But when you handle errors gracefully, your programs become much more user-friendly. Think of error handling as a safety net—it allows you to write code that's robust, reliable, and smooth.

Wrapping Up

Error handling is a critical part of becoming a confident coder. It's like having a backup plan for when things don't go as expected, ensuring that your code doesn't crash or leave users confused. From dealing with invalid inputs to handling unexpected situations, **try-except** blocks allow you to create programs that can manage mistakes gracefully.

In the next chapter, we'll dive into the world of **external libraries**, where you'll learn how to extend your Python programs with additional features!

Key Takeaways:

- Errors are common in coding, and handling them properly is essential.

- **Try-Except** blocks help catch and manage errors, preventing program crashes.

- Always remember to clean up with **finally**, even if everything runs smoothly.

- Using relatable real-life situations, like chai-making disasters or payment failures, can make understanding error handling much easier.

## Chapter 11

Introduction to External Libraries

Imagine you're trying to make a special dish for a family gathering. You could start from scratch, chopping veggies, grinding spices, and doing everything by hand, or you could grab some ready-made spice mixes and pre-chopped ingredients to speed up the process. In coding, this is exactly what external libraries do for you—they provide pre-written code that you can use to save time and effort.

In this chapter, we'll dive into the world of external libraries in Python. You'll learn what libraries are, how to install them, and how they can simplify your coding life. We'll also take a look at some fun and useful libraries that can make your programs more powerful.

What Are Libraries?

A library is a collection of pre-written code that you can use to perform common tasks without having to write the code yourself. Think of it as a set of ready-to-use tools, like a Swiss Army knife for coding. Libraries are written by other programmers and made available for everyone to use.

For example, if you want to work with dates, generate random numbers, or even create a game, there's likely a library that already has the code written for you. All you need to do is "import" it into your project and start using it.

Analogy: Cooking with a Recipe

Using a library in Python is like following a cooking recipe. You don't need to figure out every little detail—like how to grind the spices or where to source the ingredients—

because the recipe (library) has already done the heavy lifting for you. You simply follow the steps, and boom, delicious food (or in our case, working code) is ready.

How to Use External Libraries in Python

Python comes with a standard library that includes many useful modules like `math` for mathematics, `datetime` for handling dates, and `random` for generating random numbers. However, to unlock even more features, you can install external libraries written by the global Python community.

Step 1: Installing Libraries with pip

To use external libraries, you'll need to install them first. Thankfully, Python makes this easy with pip, a package installer that lets you download and install libraries with just one command.

Here's how you can do it:

1. Open your terminal or command prompt:

If you're using VS Code, open the terminal inside the editor by going to **View > Terminal**.

2. Type the following command to install a library:

```
pip install <library-name>
```

For example, if you want to install a popular library for working with web data, called **requests**, you would type:

```
pip install requests
```

3. **Wait for the installation to complete.**

   It usually takes just a few seconds, depending on your internet speed.

A Fun Example: Using the Random Library

Let's try using an external library that comes with Python's standard package: the `random` library. This library allows you to generate random numbers, shuffle lists, and even simulate rolling dice!

Here's how you can use it:

```
import random

# Simulate rolling a 6-sided dice
dice_roll = random.randint(1, 6)
print(f"You rolled a {dice_roll}!")
```

Try running this code, and every time you do, you'll get a different number between 1 and 6, just like rolling a physical dice. The `random` library saves you the trouble of having to code your own random number generator!

Installing External Libraries: A Step-by-Step Guide

Now, let's go beyond the standard libraries. We'll install an external library and use it. Let's say you want to work with **beautifulsoup4**, a library that helps you scrape data from websites (perfect for gathering information online).

Here's how you can install it:

1. **Open the terminal or command prompt:**

    If you're using VS Code, open the terminal inside the editor by going to View > Terminal.

2. **Install the library:**

```
pip install beautifulsoup4
```

3. Wait for the installation to complete. It might take a few seconds.

    Once the installation is done, you can start using the library in your project:

```python
from bs4 import BeautifulSoup
import requests

# Get the content of a web page
response = requests.get("https://
example.com")
soup = BeautifulSoup(response.
content, "html.parser")


# Print the title of the web page
print(soup.title)
```

This is a simple example that fetches the content of a webpage and prints its title. Don't worry if this seems complex for now; the point here is to show how external libraries can help you accomplish tasks that would otherwise take a lot more effort.

Why Use External Libraries?

Libraries save you time and effort, allowing you to focus on the parts of the program that matter to you most. Instead of reinventing the wheel every time, you can rely on a library to do the heavy lifting for you.

Some Popular Libraries in Python:

- **NumPy**: For scientific computing and working with arrays.

- **Pandas**: For data manipulation and analysis (think of it as Excel for Python).

- **Matplotlib**: For creating visualizations and charts.

- **Flask**: For building web applications.

- **Pillow**: For working with images.

- **PyGame**: For creating simple games.

Each of these libraries can open up new possibilities for what you can build with Python. Want to create a game? Use PyGame. Want to analyze data? Pandas is your friend.

Using Libraries Responsibly

Just like how you'd trust a well-known cookbook over a random recipe from an unknown source, it's important to use trusted libraries from reputable sources. Always check that a library is well-documented and widely used before incorporating it into your project.

Final Thoughts

External libraries are like magical shortcuts that make your coding life easier and more enjoyable. Whether you're rolling virtual dice or scraping the web for data, libraries unlock new powers in your code. The more you explore them, the more versatile your programming becomes.

In the next chapter, we'll take everything you've learned so far and apply it to a fun project—creating a simple quiz application using everything we've covered, including external libraries.

Key Takeaways:

- Libraries are pre-written code that helps you perform tasks more easily.

- Python's `pip` command allows you to install external libraries quickly.

- You can use libraries like `random`, `requests`, and `BeautifulSoup` to add new features to your programs.

- Always use libraries from trusted sources to ensure your code remains secure and reliable.

## Chapter 12

Final Project: Build a Simple Application

Welcome to the final chapter! We've walked through many fundamental programming concepts, from variables to loops, and now it's time to bring it all together. There's no better way to wrap up your learning than by building your very first Python project.

In this chapter, I'll guide you step-by-step through the creation of a simple quiz program. Think of it as your coding graduation party! By the end, you'll have a working project that showcases your newfound skills and gives you a solid foundation to build upon.

What You'll Build: A Simple Quiz Program

The project we're going to build is a basic quiz application. The user will answer a series of multiple-choice questions, and the program will keep track of their score. This may sound simple, but it incorporates many of the core principles you've learned throughout this book. Plus, you can always expand on it with new features later!

We'll cover:

- How to structure your program logically

- Using variables, loops, and conditionals to create the quiz flow

- Handling user input

- Calculating and displaying the user's score

- How to make the program flexible for any number of questions

Step 1: Outlining the Program

Before diving into the code, it's important to have a clear understanding of what our program will do. A good habit is to outline the logic first, which makes coding easier.

Here's the plan for the quiz program:

1. Display a welcome message.

2. Ask the user multiple-choice questions one by one.

3. Record the user's answer.

4. After each question, let the user know if they got it right or wrong.

5. Keep a running tally of their correct answers.

6. At the end, display the user's final score.

Step 2: Writing the Code

Now let's break it down into Python code.

1. Displaying the Welcome Message

We'll start by greeting the user and letting them know how the quiz works.

```python
print("Welcome to the Python
Quiz!")

print("You'll be asked 5 questions.
Let's see how many you get
right!\n")
```

2. Setting Up the Questions

To keep things simple, we'll use a Python list to store our questions and another list for the possible answers.

```python
questions = [
    "What is the capital of India?",
    "Who is known as the Father of
    Computers?",
    "Which Python keyword is used to define
    a function?",
    "What symbol is used for comments in
    Python?",
    "Which data type would you use to
    store True or False?"
    ]
options = [
    ["A. Mumbai", "B. New Delhi", "C.
    Bengaluru", "D. Kolkata"],
    ["A. Charles Babbage", "B. Alan
    Turing", "C. Thomas Edison", "D.
    Nikola Tesla"],
    ["A. def", "B. func", "C. function",
    "D. define"],
    ["A. //", "B. #", "C. /*", "D. --"],
    ["A. int", "B. bool", "C. str", "D.
    float"]
    ]
answers = ["B", "A", "A", "B", "B"]   #
Correct answers
```

3. Looping Through the Questions

Now, we'll use a loop to go through each question, display the options, and take user input.

```python
score = 0  # Variable to keep track
of correct answers


for i in range(len(questions)):
    print(f"Q{i+1}: {questions[i]}")
    for option in options[i]:
        print(option)
    answer = input("Your answer (A,
B, C, or D): ").upper()


    if answer == answers[i]:
        print("Correct!\n")
        score += 1
    else:
        print(f"Wrong! The correct
answer was {answers[i]}.\n")
```

4. Displaying the Final Score

At the end of the quiz, we'll display the user's total score and give them a short congratulatory message.

```python
print(f"Quiz completed! Your
final score is {score} out of
{len(questions)}.")
    if score == len(questions):
        print("Excellent! You
nailed it!")
    elif score >= 3:
        print("Good job! You're
getting there.")
    else:
        print("Don't worry,
practice makes perfect. Keep
learning!")
```

Step 3: Expanding the Project

The beauty of programming is that you can always expand and improve your projects. Here are a few ideas to take your quiz program to the next level:

- **Add More Questions**: You can easily expand the list of questions and options.

- **Add Difficulty Levels**: Create a "difficulty" mode where the quiz adapts based on user performance.

- **Randomize the Questions**: Use Python's random module to shuffle the questions so they appear in a different order each time.

- **Track High Scores**: You could save the highest scores using files, so users can compete against themselves.

- **Create a Timer**: Add a timer that tracks how long it takes the user to finish the quiz.

Conclusion

Congratulations! You've just built your very first Python project. Completing this quiz program is an important milestone in your programming journey. Not only have you learned how to work with Python code, but you've also applied logical thinking and problem-solving to create something fun and functional.

Remember, every great programmer started somewhere, and projects like this are stepping stones to more advanced skills. Keep experimenting, keep building, and soon you'll find yourself creating even more complex applications.

Celebrating Success: Your Journey Begins Here

You've done it! You've walked through the core concepts of programming, built your first Python project, and navigated the foundational principles of coding. This is a big moment. Take a second to pat yourself on the back because what you've accomplished is no small feat. Remember when you started, maybe feeling a bit unsure, wondering if coding was something you could actually do? Well, look at you now—writing code, solving problems, and creating programs. You've proven that **you can do this**.

But, here's the thing—this is just the beginning.

The Power of Patience and Perseverance

If there's one truth that applies to coding (and life), it's this: **Success doesn't happen overnight**. Every line of code you write, every error you fix, every challenge you face is part of a much bigger journey. It takes time, patience, and an unwavering sense of perseverance to become truly skilled. You'll encounter moments of frustration when things don't work the way you want them to, and times when you're stuck on a problem for hours. **That's normal**. It happens to every coder, from beginners to experts.

What separates those who succeed from those who give up is simple: they **keep going**. They don't stop because it's hard. They push through, learn from mistakes, and come out stronger on the other side. The skills you've learned in this book aren't just about coding; they're about learning how to approach problems, how to think logically, and how to stay patient in the face of challenges. These are skills that will serve you in every area of life.

You Are Capable of Anything

As you move forward in your programming journey, always remember this: **You are capable of anything you set your mind to**. There's nothing special or extraordinary that separates the top programmers in the world from you. The only difference is that they've put in the time and effort. They've kept learning, kept experimenting, and kept pushing through obstacles.

You've already shown that you have what it takes. You've embraced the world of code, learned its language, and created something from nothing. That's the heart of programming—turning ideas into reality. As you keep growing, you'll realize that the limits of what you can achieve are only as big as your imagination.

A Message for the Road Ahead

As you close this book, here's one final message I want you to carry with you:

Every great coder, every successful person in any field, started where you are right now. They weren't born knowing how to code. They didn't have all the answers at first. But they started. They learned. They failed. And then they kept going. That's the secret—just keep going.

Don't be afraid to make mistakes. Don't be discouraged by setbacks. Embrace them as part of the process. Each misstep is a stepping stone, and each failure is a lesson. With enough time, patience, and determination, you can and will achieve your goals.

What's Next? Dive into Object-Oriented Programming!

The fire you've ignited through this book—the curiosity, the excitement, the desire to learn—don't let it die out. Whether you choose to continue with coding or apply the problem-solving mindset to other areas of your life, keep that spark alive.

And if you've enjoyed this journey into programming, get ready for the next step! In my upcoming book, **"Code with Objects: A Fun Guide to Object-Oriented Programming,"** we'll dive even deeper into the world of programming. I'll walk you through the exciting principles of object-oriented programming in a way that's as fun and easy as what we've done so far. It's all about taking your skills to the next level without overwhelming you, and I promise it'll be just as engaging as this one.

Keep the Fire Burning

So, go out there and build something amazing. The future is yours to create. And remember, this is only the beginning—there's a whole new world of code waiting for you.

See you in the next book!

Acknowledgements

As I reflect on the journey that led to the creation of this book, I am filled with gratitude for the incredible people who have supported me along the way.

First and foremost, I would like to thank my dad, whose unwavering encouragement and belief in my potential inspired me to pursue my dreams relentlessly. To my mother, your love and support have been the foundation of my strength. To my brother, thank you for being my confidant and for always cheering me on.

I am deeply grateful to my friends, whose companionship and motivation kept me going through challenges.

Last but not least, to my wife, thank you for believing in me and standing by my side through every high and low. Your faith has been my guiding light. And to my son, Ayushman, you are a pure bundle of joy and my ultimate stress buster. Your laughter and innocence remind me of the beauty in life and the importance of chasing my dreams.

Each of you has played a vital role in my journey, and I am forever grateful.

Thank you for being part of this adventure.

About the Author

Growing up, life wasn't easy for us. We were a middle-class family, and like many others, we didn't have a lot of extra money for luxuries. But even though we didn't have much, we had each other—and that made all the difference.

When I was five years old, one Sunday morning, my dad and I were on our usual walk, just like every weekend. We strolled down the streets when something new caught my eye. Across the road, there was a shop with a sign that read "*Computers & More.*" It wasn't the bakery or toy store we usually passed—this was different. I had never seen anything like it before.

Through the big shop window, I could see people sitting in front of glowing screens, their fingers tapping away on keyboards. To me, it looked like magic—these strange machines, responding to people's commands as if they were alive. I didn't understand what was happening, but I was completely hooked. That was the moment something sparked inside me—a curiosity that would only grow stronger.

Unfortunately, computers were way out of our reach back then. They were expensive, and my family had to focus on more important things—making sure we had food on the table and that my brother and I got a good education. But the dream of coding never left me.

When I was 9 years old, my school finally introduced a computer class. The moment I heard about it, I practically begged my dad to let me join. It was a huge ask, though. We didn't have much money to spare—everything we had was for the essentials. But my dad, seeing how much this meant to me, found a way to make it happen. I know it wasn't easy for him—every rupee counted—but he still made sure I could take the class. For that, I'll always be deeply grateful.

In that class, I met Mr. Ganguly, my computer teacher. He must have seen something in me because he always went the extra mile to make sure I understood what we were learning. He introduced us to coding with something called GW-Basic, and while I didn't get everything right away, I loved it.

Mr. Ganguly was a marvel when it came to typing; he could fly across the keyboard with a speed and precision that left everyone in awe. Watching him type was like witnessing a master musician at work—the rhythm, the flow, and the absolute focus. I admired his skill immensely and longed to type like him. However, my chances to practice were limited.

At home, I didn't have a computer, which made it difficult to hone my skills. Our school offered computer classes on Fridays, but the logistics were challenging. With more than 50 students in the class and only eight computers in the machine room, our teacher had to devise a system. He divided the class by roll numbers: one week, the first half would get to practice in the machine room, while the other half attended theory lessons. The following week, we would switch places.

While I appreciated the opportunity, I often felt frustrated by the long wait between my practice sessions. So, one Friday, when it was my turn for theory class, I decided I couldn't let another week slip by without practicing. I carefully plotted my move.

As the class settled into the theory lesson, I noticed that a few students were particularly distracted. Seizing the moment, I quietly slipped out of the classroom and made my way to the machine room. Heart racing, I could already imagine Mr. Ganguly's fingers dancing across the keys as I envisioned my own fingers mimicking his skill.

When I entered the machine room, I felt a rush of excitement mixed with anxiety. The faint hum of the computers greeted me as I rushed to the nearest keyboard. I quickly logged in, my fingers trembling with anticipation. I started typing, trying to channel the essence of Mr. Ganguly. For those precious moments, it felt like I was flying; I typed with a fervor that was fueled by my determination to become as fast as him.

Before I could get caught, I had a sudden burst of inspiration. I grabbed a piece of paper and began to draw the entire keyboard layout. Every key, every letter, meticulously sketched out. I realized this would allow me to practice typing at home, even without a computer, helping me remember the positions of the keys and the flow of typing. I felt a surge of pride as I finished the layout; it was my little secret weapon to overcome the challenges of my limited access to practice.

But just as I was about to log out, I heard footsteps approaching. Panic surged through me. I quickly logged out and scrambled to leave the room, clutching my precious drawing. I barely made it back before the teacher noticed I was missing, but my heart swelled with pride. I had practiced, even if just for a few minutes, and I now had a plan to keep improving on my own. With my hand-drawn keyboard layout in tow, I felt like I had taken a significant step toward achieving my goal of typing as swiftly as Mr. Ganguly.

One day, my dad surprised me with a gift that would change everything. I had been pouring my heart and soul into practicing typing on that piece of paper. I'd often sit in a quiet corner, pretending to type out stories and letters, my imagination running wild with the words I could one day write. I didn't know my dad had noticed my determination and passion.

When he walked in, there was a gleam of excitement in his eyes, and in his hands, he held a keyboard. A broken, beat-up keyboard that he had found in a local computer repair shop. To most it was a piece of trash, but for me, it was pure gold! The moment I saw it, my heart raced with a mix of confusion and joy. I couldn't believe he had brought it home for me.

"I found this for you," he said, a proud smile on his face. "I know how much you love typing. Even if it's not working, you can practice on it. Just imagine the words you can type."

I stared at the keyboard, and I felt a wave of gratitude wash over me. I understood that my dad saw something in my eyes—a spark of passion and determination that I hadn't fully recognized in myself. He must have realized that I was eager to improve, that I was willing to put in the effort, even if it meant practicing on a broken keyboard. I felt like I had been given a golden ticket to my dreams. Even though it wouldn't connect to a computer, it was perfect for me. I could touch the keys, practice my form, and immerse myself in the rhythm of typing.

That broken keyboard became one of the most precious gifts I could ever receive—a symbol of my dad's understanding of my aspirations. He believed in me when I was still figuring things out, and that faith motivated me even more. From that day forward, I devoted myself to my practice, knowing that I had a tangible reminder of my dreams right in front of me. My dad's thoughtful gesture instilled in me the belief that with hard work, I could turn my passion into something extraordinary.

And then there's my brother—my hero, really. My brother was the kind of kid who understood, even from a young age, that he would have to step up and support the family. He was brilliant with numbers—a true math genius. While I stayed up at night thinking about coding, he stayed up studying math. He worked hard, always driven by the goal of helping our family have a better future.

Eventually, all his hard work paid off. He landed a job at Infosys, one of the biggest tech companies in India. That was a turning point for us. With his job, our financial situation started to improve. My brother could have easily focused on his own success, but instead, he made sure to give back to our family. He's the one who bought me my very first computer when I was 19. Core 2 Duo E4400, 1 Gb of RAM, 160 Gb Hard Disk, Intel 945GCNL Motherboard, I still remember the specs as if it was yesterday!

I can't even begin to express how grateful I am for that. He knew how much I loved coding, and he made sure I had the tools I needed to pursue that dream. Without him, none of this would have been possible. I owe so much to my brother, and I can never thank him enough for everything he's done—not just for me, but for our whole family. He stood by our dad and carried the weight of our family's future on his shoulders, and because of that, we're where we are today.

That first computer opened the door to a world of endless possibilities. I practiced coding day and night, teaching myself more and more as time went on. It wasn't long before I knew that this was what I wanted to do for the rest of my life. Coding wasn't just a skill—it became my passion.

I went on to study computer science and later took on the entrepreneurial journey. I built multiple successful ventures, learning firsthand what it takes to scale a business from the ground up. Today, I take pride in empowering businesses to thrive in the digital landscape with my new venture: Microstax Technologies Pvt. Ltd., a company that specializes in building robust, high-performance digital solutions that empower businesses to thrive in the modern world. From web development and digital infrastructure to security and technology consulting, we deliver cost-effective, scalable, and reliable solutions tailored to the client's needs. Powered by Knowledge, Driven by Values, our commitment to technical excellence and ethical business practices ensures that every solution we build is both efficient and future-ready.

This book is my way of giving back. I want to share the joy, the challenge, and the satisfaction that comes from coding. If you're just starting out, remember this—it's not going to be easy. There will be struggles, and success won't come overnight. But with dedication, patience, and perseverance, you can achieve anything.

And this journey isn't over yet! If you've enjoyed learning about coding with me, stay tuned for my next book, *"Code with Objects: A Fun Guide to Object-Oriented Programming."* It'll be another exciting step in your programming journey.

Remember, I started out as a curious kid peeking through the window of a computer shop, dreaming of a world I didn't yet understand. And with the love and support of my family, especially my brother, that dream became reality. So, to you, dear reader, I say—dream big, work hard, and never stop believing in yourself. *Anything is possible.*

"A dream is not that which you see while sleeping;
it is something that does not let you sleep."
– Dr. A. P. J. Abdul Kalam

www.ingramcontent.com/pod-product-compliance
Lightning Source LLC
Chambersburg PA
CBHW062211150726
47991CB00006B/2231